Get the Prize

Nine Keys For a Life of Victory

Written & Illustrated By:
Larry Hehn

www.larryhehn.com
larry@larryhehn.com

National Library of Canada Cataloging in Publication

Hehn, Larry, 1967-
Get the prize : nine keys for a life of victory / written & illustrated by Larry Hehn.

ISBN 1-894928-26-1

1. Success--Religious aspects--Christianity. I. Title.

BV4598.2.H43 2004 248.4 C2004-900210-4

Cover design by Nikki Braun

For those who run in such a way as to get the prize,
And for those who light the way.

Acknowledgements

Only one name appears on the cover, but this was definitely not a solo effort. *Get the Prize* grew from the guidance, encouragement, example and efforts of many people. It is impossible to acknowledge individually, within these pages, everyone who has made a contribution. For those whose names are not included here, do know that you are remembered and appreciated. For those listed below, I am forever grateful. Many thanks to:

- Desmond Watson and Marianne Van Esch, for planting and tending the Chinese bamboo
- Casey Combden, for easy answers to tough questions
- Stephen Matthews, for sharing the wealth
- Donna Messer, for asking the right question
- Jamie Crookston, for pointing ahead
- Jitka (Judy) Jirku, for making a call
- Wayne Lewis, for painting a picture
- Jim Harris, for helpful hints
- Carol Chambers, chief editor and grammar queen
- Randy Van Ness, master attitude booster
- Jack Proctor, for structural support and unparalleled enthusiasm
- Tom Koloszar, for the right perspective
- Peter Graham, technical support and tweaker of fiddly bits
- Paul Graham, no relation, for an amazing foreword
- Stephanie, Matt, Zac and Jacob, for reminding me to become more like a little child
- Monique Hehn, for approving nods, tactful suggestions, good night hugs and kisses, and being the best wife any guy could ask for. I love you.
- Most of all, my Lord and Savior, for opening and closing all the right doors. All of the good parts came from you.

Contents

Foreword

In my business, I meet a lot of people with ideas that are looking for management expertise and money to back the "next best" widget, technology, or other business acquisition opportunity. In most cases, the deal does not pass first or second round of due diligence because ultimately the people behind the deal either have not sufficiently thought the concept through, or quite simply do not have the focus and fortitude to see the deal through the numerous hurdles found along the way.

I first met Larry Hehn at our church about three years ago. A year after we met, he shared his idea of this book with me. Over much coffee and pointed questions, it became clear that Larry had the focus and fortitude to see this book through to completion.

Three aspects of this book contribute to its effectiveness: first, Larry shares personal experiences that we can all relate to. He truly and honestly is trying to live each one of the concepts, principles and platitudes found in "Get the Prize"; secondly, Larry's attitude of being a student and not a teacher is refreshing when we are bombarded in the media by the guru of the day hawking the next best strategy to effortless success, wealth and all things unimaginable; and thirdly, the timeless principles that Larry shares are not his alone – "Get the Prize" is based on Biblical wisdom and truth that will change your life for the better if you seek the Truth for your life. The investment of your time spent reading and applying the principles of "Get the Prize" will generate invaluable returns in your life.

Whatever the "Prize" may be that you are striving for, whether you know exactly where you are headed and the race you are running, perhaps you have taken a tumble along the way and are not sure if you even want to continue to run the race, or perchance you don't even know where or how to start defining what your Prize should be, this book has timeless relevant applications for readers anywhere along that spectrum of life.

I would encourage you not to rush through this book. Spend time digesting each chapter and be honest with yourself. Of the nine principles outlined in these chapters, find the area in your life that most needs to change and start today to adopt these principles for yourself. You are sure to find personal change, enrichment, and growth for yourself, while at the same time having a positive impact on the lives of those around you.

D. Paul Graham

May 2003

Introduction
Get the Prize

Do you not know that in a race all the runners run, but only one gets the prize? Run in such a way as to get the prize. – 1 Corinthians 9:24

Werner Barth was one of the best teachers I ever knew. He was a wiry man with a spring in his step, a sparkle in his eye, a gravelly voice and a thick German accent. He taught me in my first two years of university, 25 years after he had taught my father at night school. His specialty was statics, potentially one of the most boring subjects on earth. Barth was probably the only person on this planet who could make statics interesting and fun to learn.

I don't know if he was passionate about statics, but Barth definitely had a passion for learning and helping others to learn. He stood on his chair, went into contortions and shared the wildest stories to help us understand the subject matter. When our class performed poorly on a test, he cancelled our regular lesson, pulled up a chair and questioned us for an hour about how he could improve his teaching methods.

At that point he had been teaching for longer than most of us had been alive. Many professors in that situation would blame the students if their results were poor, but Barth would not accept that. He was not just a teacher; he was also still a student. Even after years of learning, applying and teaching statics, he was still searching for ways to improve. What I learned in that classroom had nothing to do with statics. It had everything to do with commitment to a life of learning and growth.

I share this book with you not as a teacher, not as an authority, but as a fellow student. I openly admit that I have not mastered the principles in these pages, but have committed to learn, apply and share them every day for the rest of my life. Like Barth, I will never give in to complacency. I want to look back on my life with the knowledge that I gave my best effort every time, win or lose, and never stopped growing. I want to "run in such a way as to get the prize." How about you?

In the race of life, are you running in such a way as to get the prize? The prize may be different for every one of us, but we all share the run. Are you making the most of your talents and striving to achieve your full potential, or have you somehow been pulled off course? Are you still learning and growing, or have you settled into a mediocre comfort zone? Are you becoming the person you were meant to be, or have you somehow lost sight of the prize?

"A racehorse that consistently runs just a second faster than another horse is worth millions of dollars more. Be willing to give that extra effort that separates the winner from the one in second place." – Life's Little Instruction Book, Volume II

The principles that follow are Biblical and proven. The contents are distilled from dozens of great books, inspirational audios, seminars and relationships with successful people from all walks of life. By taking these principles to heart and applying them to your daily life, by running in such a way as to get the prize, you will open the door to untold prosperity in your spiritual life, relationships, business life and finances.

You will find thought provoking questions in every section, along with spaces to write in your answers. Take ownership of this book. Highlight key sections, take time to answer the questions, write down notes, and make it your own. It's your book. It's your life. It's your race. On your mark, get set...

Chapter 1
Choose

> *This day...I have set before you life and death, blessings and curses. Now choose life, so that you and your children may live...*
> *– Deuteronomy 30:19*

If eternal life began today, and your assignment was to keep living the way you are now, would you have trouble calling it heaven? If you were told that your life would never improve from this day forward, would you be a little disappointed? Are there areas where you haven't reached your maximum potential? Are you still on your way to becoming the best person you could possibly be?

Where you are today in your spiritual life, relationships, business life and finances is a result of the choices you have made to date. When the options offered to us are life or death, blessings or curses, the choices are simple. But most decisions in life aren't that obvious. Since the effects of our daily choices aren't always immediate and drastic, we often don't realize where they are taking us.

Could you picture flying an airplane without any navigation equipment or landmarks to guide you? At take off, you would have to aim yourself toward your destination as accurately as possible, and hope to stay on course. What would the chances be of reaching your target without any mid-course corrections? A flight of 600 miles that was off course by only one degree would miss the landing strip by more than 10 miles!

"Well, we have nowhere to land and we're out of fuel. But boy, did we make good time!"

How often have we been like that flight, thinking that we were heading in the right direction, only to find that where we are today isn't where we had hoped to be? When I stopped to examine my life five years ago, I didn't like the life I was living. I had virtually no spiritual life, very few friends, wasn't enjoying my work and had no money. Whose fault was that? If I wanted to change my life for the better, I had to start making different choices.

Where have your choices brought you, and where are they taking you? Again, where we are today, and where we will be five years from today, is a result of our daily choices. Minor choices on a daily basis add up to significant long-term results. What choices will pull us out of the rut of mediocrity, and onto the path of success? We hold the keys when we:

- Choose our attitude
- Choose our habits
- Choose our relationships

Choose Your Attitude

> *"Nothing can stop the man with the right mental attitude from achieving his goal. Nothing on earth can help the man with the wrong attitude." – Thomas Jefferson*

One day last year, my family wanted to visit the pet store at a local mall. I dropped them off at the entrance and went to run some errands in another part of town. Returning later than planned, I rushed to the mall directory to find the location of the store. Ahead of me, a lady stood only a few inches in front of the directory, slowly studying the map and blocking my view. I was in a hurry, and was upset that she could be so inconsiderate.

Then I looked down and noticed her seeing-eye dog. The only way she could read the map was if it was just inches away from her impaired eyes. My attitude suddenly changed. Would it really make a difference if I arrived at the pet store fifteen seconds later? Did I have to snap at that lady and pass my negative attitude on to her? Not at all, but before noticing her seeing-eye dog, I almost did.

It took *less* energy for me to choose an attitude of patience and understanding. That lady had a better day as a result, and so did I. So did everyone else we met that day. How often do we allow trivial things to affect our attitude in a negative way, and then pass that negative attitude on to others? Like a tiny pebble striking the surface of a pond, every day our attitude sends out ripples that affect others. Are the ripples that you send out positive or negative?

The world we encounter is a reflection of our attitude. David and Paul were both unemployed engineers when we met. David believed that the job market was on an upswing, and expected to have multiple offers within a few weeks. Paul felt that the same market was poor, and that his prospects were dim. Which person would you rather hire? Sure enough, David's attitude earned him new employment within two weeks. Paul is probably still looking for work.

I used to work in a small die shop with John and Tony. With limited resources and demanding customers, we often had to use creative methods and materials to get things done. John's approach to any new challenge was, "That won't work." Tony accepted every new challenge with enthusiasm, saying, "Let's make it work." Who do you suppose generated all of the positive results? When shop ownership changed, Tony got a 27% raise, and John got fired.

"That'll never work."

Whether our attitude is positive or negative, it becomes a mental filter as our mind searches for reasons to validate that attitude. Choose to have a miserable day, and I guarantee that you will find reasons to consider your day miserable. Choose to make today a great day, and you will find reasons to believe that today is really great. Which would you choose?

Ask yourself...

Would I rather have a positive attitude or a negative attitude?

Why?

Choose Your Habits

"Your net worth to the world is usually determined by what remains after your bad habits are subtracted from your good ones." – Benjamin Franklin

No one has ever gained 20 pounds of unwanted weight overnight. A weight gain of 20 pounds is the long-term result of daily diet and exercise habits. If I choose habits that make me gain just one ounce per day, my weight change from week to week will be barely noticeable. But after one year, I will have gained over 20 pounds. What will happen if I choose habits that cause me to *lose* just one ounce per day?

Many years ago, I met a lady who was trying to give up a long-term habit of smoking cigarettes. She was chewing nicotine gum to curb her cravings and wean herself from smoking. She assured me that, within two months, she would be over the smoking habit for good. One year passed and we met again. Yes, she was no longer smoking. But she was now addicted to the gum!

We only get rid of our old habits by replacing them with new ones. The secret is to trade in your old habits for ones that are more positive. We all have some "bad" habits that we would like to replace, but don't limit yourself. There is nothing keeping you from trading in a "good" habit for a better one. Remember, to successfully adopt a new habit, you will have to leave another habit behind.

Picture twins, Jeff and Jane. Separated at birth, they have chosen different daily habits. Jane is a long-term thinker. She exercises and maintains a healthy diet. She expands her mind by reading books and listening to educational audios. She associates with positive, ambitious, successful people. Jane plans her financial future, making sure her income always exceeds her expenses.

Jeff is concerned with instant gratification. He eats nothing but junk food, and rarely leaves the couch. He watches TV shows with laugh tracks that tell him when something is supposed to be funny. Jeff listens to the local radio station in the car, and hasn't read a book in years. He hangs out with low achievers. Jeff is an impulse shopper, regularly spending more money than he earns.

Looking at the long-term results, Jane will be healthy, energetic, informed, financially stable and on the path to success. Jeff will be overweight, sick, narrow-minded, broke and stuck in a rut. Which result would you choose? Would you agree that Jane chose life and blessings? Would you agree that Jeff chose death and curses? But looking at his daily habits, Jeff is just an average guy. He may be your brother-in-law. He may be your neighbor. He may even be *you.*

Paint a mental picture of where you want your life to be in the next five years. When everything turns out exactly the way you want, what does it look like? Think of all areas of your life. What kind of person have you become? How do you spend your time? Who do you spend your time with? What kind of shape are you in physically? Is your spiritual life in order? Where do you live? What is your financial situation?

Cut out pictures of how you want your life to turn out, write down your dreams and goals, paste them on a board and keep them in front of you daily. Set a date for achieving them. Ask yourself what you can do in the next five minutes to get closer to that vision. Would you read a book, exercise, or call a friend instead of watching TV? Would you eat an apple instead of a cheeseburger? Would you curb your impulse spending so you can save for something more worthwhile? What would you choose to do?

Ask yourself...

What do I want my life to look like in five years?

Ask yourself...

What negative habits are keeping me from reaching it?

What positive habits could replace them?

Choose Your Relationships

> *He who walks with the wise grows wise, but a companion of fools suffers harm. – Proverbs 13:20*

As a child, did your parents ever tell you to stay away from certain children because they were a bad influence? My old friend Jamie credits his success to such advice from his grade three teacher, Mrs. Larin. When he was eight years old, Jamie started to associate with "Eddie" and "Ryan" (not their real names), two underachievers who seemed to spend more time in the principal's office than in the classroom.

Although he was advanced for his age in some subjects, Jamie allowed himself to be dragged down to their level of attention and achievement. By the middle of grade four, his marks had fallen well below his potential. Even though she was no longer his teacher, Mrs. Larin found out about Jamie's poor performance. She pulled him aside in the schoolyard one day, and said, "*You* know, and *I* know, that you can do better."

She challenged him to think about where his life was headed if he kept Eddie and Ryan as his best friends. Jamie had a mental image of where he wanted to be as an adult, and realized that Eddie and Ryan's chosen path would not take him there. He wanted to reap the rewards of working to his full potential. Eddie and Ryan seemed content to quit school in their early teens and work minimum wage jobs for the rest of their lives, if they managed to stay out of jail.

That day, a nine-year old boy experienced what he now calls a "moment of clarity," and made a choice that changed his life. Jamie removed himself from the influence of his negative friends and started to associate with positive, ambitious friends. He sharpened his focus, his grades improved and his self-respect returned. Today he is a successful businessman with a young family, the result of choosing who he spent time with at an early age.

Sometimes we forget that the same principle applies to us as adults. I once met a police officer who had worked undercover for three years in a motorcycle gang. I knew that Chris had children, and innocently asked how he was able to maintain his identity of husband and father while being forced to associate with hardened criminals every day. With sadness in his voice, he told me that he wasn't successful in keeping the two separate, and it had cost him his marriage.

"No thanks, Noah. I'm staying here with my friends."

Always look for positive relationships that will help you stretch and grow. My college hockey team was one of the best in the country, twice making it to the national finals. Although they already had two talented goaltenders, I attended tryouts every year. After two weeks of training with some of the best college hockey players around, the coach called me into his office and cut me from the team.

Choosing a positive attitude, I sincerely thanked the coach for allowing me two free weeks of intense training. When I returned to play with my regular industrial league team, they were amazed at my better performance. What caused such a noticeable improvement? My two-week relationship with a professional coach and a team of gifted athletes raised my playing ability to a much higher level.

Many of my friends are content to live mediocre lives and never begin to realize their true potential. That doesn't mean that they are no longer my friends. But it does mean that I choose not to spend much time with them. I choose to spend time with friends who always strive to improve themselves and stretch my thinking in the process. Would you rather spend time with people who lift you up or people who hold you back?

Ask yourself...

Who do I spend most of my time with?

How are they challenging me to grow?

How are they holding me back?

Choose

When I married my wife, I promised to be true to her in good times and bad times, in sickness and in health. I will honor that promise for life because I am a man of my word. But given the choice, do you think that I would prefer good times rather than bad times? Would I choose health before sickness? Of course I would.

Imagine coming to a fork in the road in your life's journey. The road to the right leads to spiritual fulfillment and the road to the left leads to emptiness. Which road would you take? The right will take you to uplifting, exciting relationships while the left will lead you to stagnant, boring relationships. Which way would you turn? Success is to the right and mediocrity is to the left. Where will you go? The road to the right leads to wealth and the road to the left leads to poverty. Which would you choose?

Would anyone in their right mind choose bad times over good, sickness over health, emptiness over spiritual fulfillment, stagnant relationships over uplifting ones, mediocrity over success, or poverty over wealth? Again, when the options offered to us are life or death, blessings or curses, the choices are simple. And our daily choices, no matter how small, will lead us in one direction or the other. Set before you are life and death, blessings and curses. Which will you choose?

"Every day all of us make hundreds of choices, most of them so menial and habitual that they are almost as automatic as breathing. Those who live in unhappy failure have never exercised their options for the better things of life because they have never been aware that they had any choices." – Og Mandino

Chapter 2
Become Like Little Children

And he said, "I tell you the truth, unless you change and become like little children, you will never enter the kingdom of heaven." – Matthew 18:3

When was the last time someone told you to become like a little child? I always thought we were supposed to be *less* childish as we got older. Have we had it wrong for all these years? Should we be back in Mrs. Mooney's kindergarten class, making a pencil holder out of an old tin can, construction paper and assorted pasta? Should we be throwing a temper tantrum in the middle of the grocery store if our spouse doesn't buy our favorite cereal? Is it safe for someone our size to use a seesaw?

What does it *really* mean to change and become like little children? What do little children do that we as adults have stopped doing, and what are the benefits? Children ask questions, learn new ideas and develop new skills. They increase their relationships, explore and embrace a world of endless possibilities. They are naturally curious, and constantly seek out new challenges and opportunities. Think about it; every year children *grow*!

Two of the most rewarding things we have done with our children were to shoot home videos of them and take them for professional portraits every year. It is so much fun to look back and see how tiny they were, hear how squeaky their voices were, and listen to them developing their vocabulary. I also enjoy laying out their portraits in chronological order and seeing the changes they have gone through over the years.

It is easy to spot the growth from year to year in children. But if we looked back one, two, five years in your life, would we be able to see the growth in you? Where is it written that, as we approach adulthood, we have to lose the desire to learn, explore and stretch our horizons? Who said that we have to settle for a life of mediocrity and boredom?

What's holding us back from running as to get the prize? What's keeping us from a life of significance? What key areas can we focus on to dramatically improve our spiritual life, relationships, business life and finances? Again, what do little children do that we as adults have stopped doing?

- Children acknowledge their own weakness
- Children adapt
- Children persist

Acknowledge Your Weakness

> *"The acknowledgement of our weakness is the first step in repairing our loss."*
> *– Thomas a Kempis*

Little children - especially babies - eagerly let the whole world know when they need attention. They cry when they are hungry, thirsty, wet, cold, hurt or lonely. Their survival depends on it. Can you imagine what would happen to a baby if it weren't able to communicate its needs? Or even worse, what if the baby chose not to communicate its needs?

Picture an infant in a basket, abandoned on the orphanage doorstep. She is hungry, cold and in need of a fresh diaper. She wants to be brought inside, fed and changed but doesn't cry because she refuses to acknowledge her weakness. No one realizes that she is there, so she sits in the basket and quietly suffers. Would this ever happen? Of course it wouldn't.

In reality, she doesn't mind admitting that she depends on others for her survival. She cries out because she has faith that someone who cares will hear her cry for help and will fill her need. Like that baby, we position ourselves to get the prize only when we admit that we have weaknesses and, more importantly, need help to overcome them.

What can happen to us as adults when we refuse to acknowledge our weakness? Several years ago, my wife and I bought a heavy four piece oak wall unit. At the time, I recognized that the people at the furniture store were much more qualified to deliver and assemble it than I was. Yes, it cost us a few dollars more, but it was brought in and assembled without a scratch, and without any effort on our part.

A few years later, we decided to move the wall unit from one room to another. I noticed a little warning sticker that said at least two people should be present when moving the unit. It was sound advice, but I didn't feel like waiting for someone else to show up. Ignoring the warning, I started to dismantle it by myself and quickly found out why the warning sticker was there. On a happy note, we still have three out of four pieces, no stitches were required, and I learned a valuable lesson.

"May I help you now?"

I am weak at fixing my car, so I take it to a mechanic. I am weak at cutting my own hair, so I visit the barber. I am weak at diagnosing illnesses, so I see my doctor. Should you feel ashamed that you aren't as skilled as a doctor, a licensed mechanic or even a barber in their field of expertise? Of course you shouldn't. So why are we reluctant to seek help when we are struggling with our spiritual life, relationships with family and friends, our business life or our finances?

Michael Jordan dominated the sport of basketball, but without teammates his club would have lost every game. Wayne Gretzky was the greatest point scorer in National Hockey League history, but without a goalie and four other skaters on the ice, his team never would have won.

Michael Jordan and Wayne Gretzky brought success to their team by focusing on their own strengths and allowing their teammates to support them in their weak areas.

We all have weaknesses and, frankly, some of them will never go away. Just as you would seek out a mechanic to fix a car problem, or a doctor to take care of a medical problem, seek out someone who can support you in the area of your weakness. Make life a team sport, humble yourself like a little child, and ask for help. Admitting that we are dependent on others for our success opens us up to an abundance of insight and blessings.

Ask yourself…

What are my weaknesses?

Whose strengths could I employ to support me in those areas?

Ask yourself...

What are my strengths?

Who could employ them for their own support?

Adapt

> *"When you're finished changing, you're finished." - Benjamin Franklin*

I remember seeing a television news feature on Tiger Woods when he was nine years old. Probably the only reason I remembered the feature was his unusual name. He was already raising eyebrows with his ability on the golf course, and I recall wondering if we would hear from young Tiger in the future, or if he would be one of those child stars who never lived up to early expectations.

Why did Tiger Woods continue to succeed while so many child stars do not? When most of us experience a certain level of success, we tend to grow dependent on the skills that got us to that level. Unfortunately, the skills that got us to that level are the same ones that *keep* us at that level. To improve, we need to adapt the skills we use. Tiger Woods was an excellent golfer when he was nine years old. However, to raise his level of play to that of the professional tour, he had to adapt.

I recently spoke with Jim Harris, author of *The Learning Paradox*. His book illustrates the need for businesses to adapt and change their thinking in order to survive. He compared life to a video game, in which we must master a certain set of skills to progress from one level to the next. Each subsequent level presents us with a new set of challenges, often requiring a different set of skills, or at least a different approach, to succeed.

I learned about that firsthand when I tried to play some of the video games that my children enjoy. Of the games I tried, only one appealed to me because I was moderately successful right away. I didn't have to change my thinking or my methods drastically, and didn't need to ask our four-year old son for help. Needless to say, that was the game that my children hardly ever played, because they conquered it right away and found it boring.

Why did I stick with the comfortable and familiar, while they eagerly graduated from one game to another? Children are willing to adapt, tackling new video games with enthusiasm, often progressing strictly through trial and error. With each level, they learn and modify their style to beat their personal best. I stuck with the one familiar game, because I could do it well and didn't have to stretch to succeed.

Sadly, that same approach is not limited to video games. How often do we hide from new technology, new ideas, new challenges and new opportunities for growth? In the video game of life, have you reached a plateau? Are you spending your days stuck in level three because you know you'll have to stretch beyond your comfort zone to tackle level four? Are you playing the old, familiar game when you should be moving on? What would your children do in the same situation?

Ask yourself...

What skills have brought me success to date?

What changes must I make to progress to the next level of achievement?

Persist

> *...for though a righteous man falls seven times, he rises again...*
> *- Proverbs 24:16*

My parents filmed home movies of me when I was three years old. With a brightly colored sweater and an oversized plastic driver and ball, young Larry tackled the vast golf course of Mom and Dad's back yard. After a quick glance at the camera, he checked his stance and took a mighty swing. Swish! He missed the ball completely. Whiff! The ball stayed put. Thud. Oops, a little too close to the ground. Swoosh! Getting closer, now...

Not once did he show any sign of giving up. Finally on the fifth swing, plink! The ball sailed straight up the fairway for a drive of four yards. Pleased as could be, he made his way to the ball and started again. Swish! Whiff! Thud... I don't know for sure, but I bet Tiger Woods started playing golf exactly the same way. How did he become the top player in golf while I still struggle to break 100?

At some point between my childhood and today, I got frustrated with the shortcomings of my golf game and gave up. Today I play golf about once every three years, get discouraged and wait another three years to try again. If I continue that pattern, I can expect to always be a poor golfer. Tiger Woods, on the other hand, chose to persist. With each swing he learned, adjusted and raised his golf game to new levels.

Watch a child as he takes his first steps. He could fall a thousand times as he learns to walk. Rather than consider his falls a sign of failure, he accepts them as part of the learning process. Falling isn't comfortable, but he persists and becomes more fulfilled and productive as a result. He learns with each fall, adjusts and improves his ability to walk until it finally becomes second nature.

"Forget it, Josh. I tried walking once. It doesn't work."

Michael Jordan was cut from his high school basketball team in his sophomore year. A newspaper editor once fired Walt Disney because he "lacked creativity". Thomas Edison worked for almost two years, making several thousand attempts, to invent the light bulb. Just like all these high achievers, we only grow by persisting through tough challenges.

What limits have you placed on your life by quitting, or not even trying, something that goes beyond your level of comfort? Many of us have convinced ourselves to settle for a mediocre lifestyle rather than face the discomfort of stretching for what we are truly called to become. How will you feel about yourself when you step up and do something great with your life?

We weren't put on this earth just to take up space for several decades. Inside each of us is the potential to have a positive impact on thousands of lives. The only thing standing between you and a life of significance is the decision to step out on faith and persist. Remember, NFL great Walter Payton was knocked down every thirteen feet, but over his career he ran the football for a total of nine and a half miles! How far will you go, if you simply persist?

Ask yourself...

What would I attempt in my life if I knew I couldn't fail?

Become Like Little Children

As we progress through school we are encouraged to be independent thinkers, to find answers on our own. Emphasis is placed on our weak subjects and we are told to focus on improving our results in those areas. We are taught to develop our weaknesses rather than our strengths. Can you imagine how silly it would have been to ask Wayne Gretzky to improve his goaltending skills, since he already was good at scoring on the other team?

Contrary to popular belief, life is a team sport. We all have weaknesses and we all have strengths. One of the keys to getting the prize is to use our strengths and join with others whose strengths support our areas of weakness. Children aren't afraid to ask for help. Children stretch beyond their comfort zone. Children never stop learning, adjusting and improving. When will you change and become like a little child?

"It is not the critic who counts; not the man who points out how the strong man stumbled or where the doer of deeds could have done them better. The credit belongs to the man who is actually in the arena, whose face is marred by dust and sweat and blood; who strives valiantly; who errs and comes short again and again; who knows great enthusiasms, the great devotions; who spends himself in a worthy cause; who at the best, knows in the end the triumph of high achievement, and who, at the worst, if he fails, at least fails while daring greatly so that his place shall never be with those timid souls who know neither victory or defeat." - Theodore Roosevelt

Chapter 3
Ask

> *"Ask and it will be given to you; seek and you will find; knock and the door will be opened to you." – Matthew 7:7*

The hockey season was about to start and our team still needed a goalie. Our coaches asked us, a room full of nine-year-old boys, if we had any volunteers. While I sat there thinking about it, one of the boys on the other side of the dressing room raised his hand. I also wanted to try playing goal, but I was too shy to raise my hand. As the only volunteer, Frank became our full time goaltender.

Six years later, I again found myself on a team that needed a goalie. Our regular goaltender had a bad habit of not showing up for games, and of playing very poorly when he did. This time I wasn't too shy. I asked the coach if I could fill in for Pat whenever he didn't show up. My team played well in front of me, and the following season I became our full time goalie. At the year-end banquet, I was given the league's "Most Improved Player" award.

Even with such a late start, I became an above average goalie by the time I was in my early twenties. I loved to play goal, and it showed. How much better could I have been if I had started at age nine? Anyone who has seen me play knows that I probably wasn't blessed with enough raw talent to become a professional goalie, but an extra seven years of coaching and practice would have made me a much better goaltender than I ever became. I missed the first opportunity simply because I didn't ask for it.

My mother has always tried to protect me from disappointment. I remember through high school and college, she encouraged me not to ask the most attractive girl in the class out for a date. I was never the most handsome, athletic or charming guy in the room, and she wanted to save me from certain rejection. She actually encouraged me to ask out the homely girls, since she figured that they would appreciate the attention. Plus, if they said no, it wouldn't be such a devastating loss for me.

I'm glad that I never heeded my mother's advice in that case. I still asked the attractive girls for dates, and dealt with frequent rejection. Sometimes one of them would accept my offer, and that made it all worthwhile. I can look back on my dating years with absolutely no regrets because I asked every girl that I wanted to ask. I never wondered what might have been, if I only had been courageous enough to ask for that date.

I asked my wife to marry me after knowing her for only three weeks. We were almost inseparable since we first met, and I knew that we were meant to be together for life. Why take any chances? Sure, I opened myself up to possible rejection by asking for her hand in marriage so soon, but I also opened myself up to her acceptance. I knew that we would never get married unless I asked.

By proposing in the middle of a crowded university pub, I got to marry the woman of my dreams. By not raising my hand in that dressing room, I missed the chance to excel at my favorite sport. Have you missed opportunities in your spiritual life, relationships, business life and finances by not asking for them? If you don't ask, you don't get. Keep these three keys in mind:

- Ask the right questions
- Ask big
- Ask often

Ask the Right Questions

"Always the beautiful answer who asks a more beautiful question." – E.E. Cummings

A few years ago, I worked for a company whose sales were falling dramatically. Our Director of Sales called a meeting to address the concerns of one very picky client. We sat around the boardroom, trying to figure out what we were doing wrong. We focused on our mistakes and where we were letting our customer down. There was no energy in the room at all; everyone seemed crushed and defeated. No wonder it wasn't a positive experience. We were asking ourselves the wrong questions!

We asked ourselves what we were doing wrong. We asked ourselves where we were disappointing our customer. We spent so much time focusing on the negative that we had no room for solutions. Things only improved when we started asking ourselves what we were doing right. We looked at the positive things we were doing, and asked what other positive things we could do for our customer.

Our situation hadn't changed, but the questions we asked got us different answers, answers that we could take and apply for positive results. Instead of asking yourself why you are overweight, ask what you can do to lose a few pounds. Instead of asking why you are broke, ask what you can do to make some extra money, or lower your expenses. Ask a question that gives you a positive answer, with positive applications.

"Why don't people take me seriously?"

Early astronomers assumed that the earth was the center of the universe. They observed the movement of the other planets and the stars across the sky and asked themselves, "How exactly do those things revolve around the earth?" By making a wrong assumption, they asked the wrong questions. By seeking answers to the wrong questions, they ensured that they would never discover the truth.

Copernicus asked a better question than the other astronomers. Rather than ask, "How do the planets and stars revolve around the earth?" he simply asked, "How do the planets and stars move?" By asking the right questions, he opened the door to the right answers. At first his answers were rejected, because they went against popular opinion. But today we know and accept that the earth is not the center of the universe.

Just like the early astronomers, you can stop your own progress by asking the wrong question. When I wanted to break out of debt and earn a larger income, the first question I asked myself was how I could find a better job. That was the wrong question, since it assumed that the answer to my financial challenges was another job. Is a better job the right answer? Is the earth the center of the universe?

When I finally asked the right question – what did I need to do to break out of debt and earn a larger income – the answer was to leave the "security" of working for someone else for a weekly paycheck and to go out on my own and learn to become a business owner. I nearly rejected that answer, since it went against popular opinion. It meant leaving my comfort zone. In the end, though, it was the right answer for me. Have popular opinion and the fear of leaving your comfort zone kept you from asking the right questions? By asking the right questions, we get the right answers. By applying the right answers, we get to where we want to be.

Ask yourself...

What are the right questions for me to ask?

Am I ready to accept and apply the right answers?

Ask Big

> *"You see things as they are and ask, 'Why?' I dream things as they never were and ask, 'Why not?'" – George Bernard Shaw*

We can learn a lot from children about asking big, especially when it comes to Christmas presents. Every year our children pounce on the Christmas catalogs, cutting things out, circling items with markers, writing down stock numbers. They scamper up to us with lists as long as their arm and inform us of their daily revisions. They know that they won't get everything on their list, but they are positioning themselves to win.

Doesn't that make sense? By asking big, you position yourself to win. Which is better, asking for three cookies and settling for two, or asking for one cookie and getting exactly what you asked for? My wife understands this completely. Early in our marriage, she didn't realize that I took asking quite literally. When she mentioned that she really didn't need any Christmas presents one year, I respected her wishes and got her...absolutely nothing for Christmas.

After regaining consciousness, I realized that even when your wife says that you don't need to get her anything for Christmas, you should get her something anyway. My wife learned that it is a good idea to ask big, especially if you have a cheap husband. Now when Christmas draws near, she gives me a list of five possible gifts that she would like to receive. We both know that at least one of them will be under the tree on Christmas morning!

Most of us have been conditioned to limit our asking to what seems realistic or polite. As an employee, I worked my way up the corporate ladder by jumping from opportunity to opportunity. Whenever I went for a job interview, friends and relatives cautioned me not to ask for too large a salary, since that might keep me from getting the job. Sadly, I heeded their advice and made a habit of securing jobs that wouldn't pay my bills. How smart was that?

As a rookie consultant I was concerned that my rates were too high until I spoke to my brother-in-law. The first thing he said to me was, "Your rates are far too..." and I cringed, waiting to hear the word "high". Imagine my surprise when he finished his sentence with the word "low"! He showed me that I was selling myself short. My clients were willing to pay top dollar for my services because I gave them good value for their money. All I had to do was ask.

Of course, asking big is not all about material things. Ask big for opportunities in your spiritual life, relationships, business life and finances. Whether you ask big or small, the worst that can happen is that you'll be given less than you asked for. Would you rather settle for less of small or less of big? When you ask big, you just might receive big. When you ask small, you guarantee that you'll never receive big. Which sounds better to you?

Ask yourself...

Would I rather receive big or small?

How big would I ask if I knew that it would be given to me?

Ask Often

> *"Who questions much, shall learn much, and retain much." – Francis Bacon*

Once again, we can learn a lot from children about asking often. With four children of our own, sometimes it feels like a fast paced game show at our house. Questions fly back and forth across the dinner table. That's fine with me, because I know that as long as they are asking questions, our children are learning and growing. No matter how many questions they ask or how often they ask, I hope that I never tire of helping them find the answers.

As we get older and more experienced, sometimes we get the idea that asking lots of questions will make us appear stupid. Have you ever held back from asking a question because someone might think that it was silly, or because you feel that you should know the answer already? By giving in to that fear, we keep ourselves from learning and growing. Chances are that someone else has the same question as you, but is also afraid to ask.

My mechanic knows that whenever I bring my car to him for repairs, I'll be asking plenty of questions. I know virtually nothing about cars, but every time I experience a new problem with our vehicle, I ask and learn something more about auto repair. When Johan calls me in to the shop, points up at part of my car and says, "Do you see that?" I have no problem saying, "Yep, I see it. What is it, and what is it supposed to look like?"

I could just sit back, nod my head and bluff my way through the conversation, but then how would I know whether or not he is telling me the truth? By asking often, I let him know that I trust him to keep me informed. By showing him that respect, I have earned his respect in return. Would you rather work with someone who asks often and makes sure that they are informed, or with someone who pretends to know more answers than they really do?

Asking often can also mean persisting with a single request. My brother-in-law must have asked my sister-in-law dozens of times to marry him. Each time she didn't feel quite ready to make the commitment, and told him no. He could have given up after her first refusal, but he knew that he just had to keep asking until the time was right. After sixteen long years of dating and countless proposals, they finally were married and now have two young children.

While developing the light bulb, Thomas Edison asked thousands of questions to lead him to the right answer. Margaret Mitchell asked more than 30 publishers before one finally said yes to publishing *Gone With the Wind.* Without asking often, Thomas Edison would never have developed the light bulb. Margaret Mitchell would never have published a book. How many times have you given up on something after asking only once?

Picture an ocean containing all of the wisdom, knowledge and opportunity that the universe has to offer. Now consider what fraction of that wisdom, knowledge and opportunity you or I have taken advantage of as an individual. Have we experienced more than one or two buckets each? It is safe to say that the amount of wisdom, knowledge and opportunity that we have *missed* far outweighs the amount that we have experienced. The only thing keeping us from the rest is asking. Why not ask often?

Ask yourself...

What opportunities are available to me?

How often have I asked for them?

Ask

We have all missed opportunities by not asking for them. Sometimes we have simply asked the wrong questions and not put ourselves in position to receive the right answers. Other times we may have sold ourselves short by asking for only what we felt we deserved or what we thought was available. We have even become discouraged and stopped asking, when all we needed to do was persist to reap the available rewards.

If we fail to ask for the opportunities or resources we need to get the prize, we have no one to blame but ourselves for our lack of success. The prize will not be handed to you; you must earn it. We bring ourselves closer to getting the prize by asking the right questions, asking big and asking often. All of the resources that you need to realize your full potential are available, waiting for you to ask. Will you?

"Indeed if we consider the unblushing promise of reward and the staggering nature of the rewards promised in the Gospels, it would seem that our Lord finds our desires not too strong, but too weak. We are half-hearted creatures like an ignorant child who wants to go on making mud pies in a slum because he cannot imagine what is meant by the offer of a holiday at the sea. We are far too easily pleased." – C. S. Lewis

Chapter 4
Commit

Commit to the Lord whatever you do, and your plans will succeed.
– Proverbs 16:3

What is commitment, anyway? Every week, couples walk down the aisle and promise themselves to each other in marriage. Every day someone decides to quit smoking, start a diet or follow an exercise plan. Yet a staggering number of marriages end in divorce. Countless diets and gym memberships are put on the shelf. We pull up short on our obligations to personal health, relationships, business ventures and financial matters.

Why are we so afraid of commitment? By definition, a commitment is an obligation that limits our choice of action. Commitment involves giving our entire self, doing whatever it takes to achieve desired results. Often "whatever it takes" involves going beyond our comfort zone. And, sad but true, once the emotion of the initial decision starts to fade and things get uncomfortable, many of us lack the integrity to follow through on what we told ourselves and others we would do.

If your spouse had only 98% commitment to your marriage, wouldn't you be upset about that other two percent? If you booked an appointment with your doctor, dentist, mechanic, hairdresser, whoever...and they didn't honor that commitment, how would you feel? Would you refer their services to any of your friends? Which pilot would you rather pay to fly your plane, one who was committed to landing safely or one who was just thinking about it?

"What do you mean, 'I guess I do?'"

Over the last couple of years, my parents and several of their peers have celebrated 50th wedding anniversaries. Over 50 years they faced financial challenges, health concerns, conflicting priorities, arguments, compromise and sacrifice. They stuck with each other not because it was easy, but because they were committed to each other and to making their marriage work. Success in any endeavor requires commitment.

Honoring our commitments is not always easy or comfortable, but the rewards are well worth the effort. Just ask the athlete who committed to years of rigorous training to earn an Olympic medal. Talk to the couple that just celebrated their 50th wedding anniversary, or the dieter who just reached her ideal weight. What commitments can we make today, to rise above mediocrity and live a life of significance?

- Commit to following your dreams
- Commit to personal growth
- Commit to action

Commit To Following Your Dreams

> *"There are some people who live in a dream world, and there are some who face reality; and then there are those who turn one into the other." – Douglas Everett*

I can't remember his name, but I'll never forget the look in his eyes. He was a successful entrepreneur who appeared to be in his early fifties, although I knew he was over 70. He had been in business for many years designing and building custom machines. I was a 24-year old employee of a small plastics company, sent to his office to help install a plastic shield and put the finishing touches on his latest invention.

As we worked together, I figured out why he seemed so young. He had spent every day pursuing his dream of working with his hands, creating innovative machines that would be useful to society. He had a reason to get up in the morning, a passion that drove him to success. He had never compromised his dreams and goals, even in the early days when money was scarce. Instead he persisted to make them a reality.

He saw more potential in me than I saw in myself at the time, and he asked if I had ever considered getting into business for myself, just as he had done many years before. I replied that I would love to, but I was almost broke, had a wife and young daughter, and was barely making enough money to live paycheck to paycheck. I couldn't pass up that "secure" income to venture out on my own and pursue my dreams.

The look of disappointment on his face still haunts me today. He knew that he was talking to someone who had already given up and was destined to live a life of mediocrity. At the age of 24 I had already shrunk my dreams down to what I could afford to do with my tiny salary. How I wish that I could find him today and let him know that a small spark of his enthusiasm stuck with me and lit a fire several years later.

We all start off with a mental picture of the way we would like things to turn out in our lives. Too often we shrink that picture down to what we can afford, or what we would be willing to settle for, or what we feel is possible based on our self-image. What does your personal definition of success *really* look like? In what areas of your life have you settled for mediocrity? What is keeping you from spending every moment expanding and chasing your dreams?

Take a few minutes and write down all of your dreams. What do you want to be, do and have? Forget about what you believe is or isn't possible, write them all down. As you grow and develop new dreams, add them to the list. Add pictures to the list and keep them in front of you every day. Set dates for when you want these things to become a reality. Again, don't limit yourself to what seems realistic. Don't weigh the possibilities based on your current situation. Dare to dream big!

How do you commit to following a dream that right now seems out of reach? Once you have set a date for when you want to achieve your dream, set benchmark goals along the way. Break your goals down to the next step that will lead you in the right direction. Then choose to spend every day working toward them. If you haven't achieved your goal by the set date, reset it and keep going. Will you see all of your dreams come true in your lifetime? I hope not. If all of your dreams come true, you haven't dreamed big enough!

Ask yourself...

What are my dreams?

Ask yourself...

What am I doing today to bring me closer to achieving them?

Commit To Personal Growth

"Employ your time in improving yourself by other men's writings so that you shall come easily by what others have labored hard for." – Socrates

Why are many lottery jackpot winners broke within two years of their windfall? What causes young "overnight successes" in professional sports or entertainment to wind up penniless after a short period of fame and fortune? The instant millionaire often does not know how to handle his new riches, and fails to develop the necessary money management skills. The same habits that made him poor in the first place will drive him back to the poor house again, no matter how much money he is given.

Often we place too much emphasis on the desired results, and not enough on the person we need to be to achieve and support those results. What if you had never jogged before and suddenly decided that you wanted to be a marathon runner; would it be reasonable to expect your body to go out tomorrow and endure a 26-mile run? In reality it would take several months of conditioning before your body was ready for such a test.

Why not take the same approach to all aspects of our lives; not just our physical body but our spiritual life, relationships, business life and finances as well? Start investing money, time and effort in your own personal development, conditioning yourself for success. The average American spends more than four hours per day watching television. What if those four hours were devoted instead to personal growth?

What if you knew that you would get one step closer to your dreams simply by investing 15 minutes or more per day in reading from a personal development book? Would you take the time on your coffee break or lunch break, get up 15 minutes earlier or simply turn off the TV and read instead? I have never met a person who owes their success to what they watched on television, but thousands of lives have been changed for the better by the right books.

If you could become better simply through listening to one motivational or educational audio per day, would it be worth the effort? Again, it's not as hard as you think. Borrow some motivational or educational audios from your local library and plug them into your stereo. Maximize your time by pressing "play" when you are driving in your car, working around the house, exercising, or even when you are in the shower. Discover the teachers and speakers who inspire you, then begin to invest in your own personal library.

Would you have the guts to discard the things in your life that are keeping you from your ultimate success? We have already learned that our chosen relationships have the potential to make us or break us. Seek out positive friends, associates and environments that will challenge you to become the person you have always dreamed of becoming. Learn from the success of others. Put yourself in situations that force you to grow and become a better person.

Be conscious of what you feed your mind, just as you are aware of what you feed your body. We invest a tremendous amount of time, money and thought into feeding, exercising and protecting our physical bodies, but rarely spend the same amount on our minds. Through the tools of personal development books, motivational and educational audios and association with successful people, we bring the prize within our grasp.

Ask yourself...

What is keeping me from reading at least 15 minutes per day from a personal development book?

What is keeping me from listening to at least one motivational or educational audio per day?

What is keeping me from associating with positive, successful people on a daily basis?

How will I overcome these obstacles?

Commit To Action

> *"Well done, is better than well said."* – *Benjamin Franklin*

There is a large vacant lot just a few blocks from my house. It is on a busy street corner, and has been undeveloped for at least ten years. It was paved many years ago, but now it is riddled with cracks and covered by large, hearty weeds. It could be cleaned up and developed into a beautiful park, valuable office space or even a much-needed service station. Right now it provides nothing of value except a short cut for pedestrians.

With a large volume of traffic driving by every day, and large numbers of people walking through the lot, sometimes it contains more than weeds. There are no public garbage containers nearby, and often you can spot some trash nestled among the plant life. Some papers are swept in by the wind, sometimes a thoughtless motorist will toss garbage out their window, and uncaring pedestrians will leave candy wrappers or other garbage behind.

I could complain to the city about that parcel of land if I wanted to. I could send letters to the mayor and city council. I could organize a rally for our neighbors to stand in front of city hall and scream for something to be done. I could write to our local newspaper about what an eyesore that piece of property is, and criticize our local government for allowing it to sit littered and unused. With all of my whining and complaining, people may see me as a person of action. But am I really?

"I work so hard to keep this city clean..."

The person of action is not the person who complains about what someone else has done or has failed to do. The person of action is the one who grabs a rake, a broom, a shovel, some gloves and a dozen garbage bags, and spends a Saturday afternoon cleaning up that lot. The person of action doesn't waste time complaining about the way things are or finding someone to blame for the situation; the person of action actually does something about it.

Have you spent more time complaining about your situation than doing something about it? Spectators and critics never get the prize; the prize goes to the person running the race. Identify your dreams. Set goals and make plans for achieving them. Then strap on your shoes and begin your race.

Ask yourself...

What do I need to do to make my dreams a reality?

Will I commit to it?

Commit

Several winters ago, my wife and I drove to a weekend business seminar in Toledo, Ohio. The trip from our home would normally take just over four hours. Unfortunately, that Friday morning we were hit with the biggest blizzard of the year. Along the highway, we passed dozens of cars and trucks that had spun off the road and into the ditch. Not only were the roads treacherous, our car's alternator died halfway through the trip.

We managed to limp into Windsor, where the car stopped completely. By then it was late Friday evening and all of the auto repair shops were closed. We had no way of getting the car fixed that day. In my mind, the only option was to stay overnight in Windsor and wait for the car to be repaired on Saturday. I allowed the driving conditions and the state of our car to determine whether or not we pressed forward to the seminar. Based on that decision, would you say that I was committed to making it to Toledo?

Thankfully, my wife was focused on our commitment rather than our comfort. She was not going to allow the weather, our crippled car or anything else to keep us from our destination. She called the local airport and arranged for a rental car. Some good Samaritans graciously loaned us a fresh car battery, hooked us up and followed us to a local garage. They then drove us over to the airport to pick up our rental car. We arrived six hours later than planned, but we made it to Toledo that night.

Do you think the other people at the seminar were impressed with the level of commitment we displayed? Our actions in that one situation demonstrated that we were serious about success, and earned many new friendships and associations that may have taken years to develop otherwise. Who would you want to be associated with, the people who used every means possible to keep their commitment to you, or those who gave up when things got rough?

What is commitment, anyway? It's pushing beyond your comfort zone. It's focusing on the prize and not the effort. It's earning the respect of others and causing untold resources to come available that you never knew existed. It's stepping out on faith and knowing that you are on your way to living a life of purpose and significance. It's the satisfaction of working toward your dreams.

"Until one is committed, there is hesitancy, the chance to draw back, always ineffectiveness. Concerning all acts of initiative (and creation) there is one elementary truth, the ignorance of which kills countless ideas and splendid plans: that the moment one definitely commits oneself, then Providence moves too. All sorts of things occur to help one that would otherwise never have occurred. A whole stream of events issues from the decision, raising in one's favor all manner of unforeseen incidents and meetings and material assistance, which no man could have dreamt would have come his way."
- W.N. Murray

What are you committed to?

Chapter 5
Do Everything

I can do everything through him who gives me strength. – Philippians 4:13

My mother makes the best carrot cake in the world. Some may try to prove me wrong, and I will gladly sample all entries to settle any dispute. Call me simple, call me unsophisticated, but it's my favorite kind of cake. When my birthday rolls around, don't bother with a fancy cheesecake or anything like that. Just park a carrot cake under that truckload of candles, and I'll be happy.

Sadly, even Mom falls short every once in a while. Once, many years ago, she served a brownish-orange slab of dense dough for dessert. It tasted like carrot cake, but looked more like astronaut food than the light, airy cake it was supposed to be. What went wrong? Was Mom trying out a new recipe for the space program? No, she simply forgot one ingredient: the baking powder. Without it, the cake was as flat as a hockey puck, and twice as heavy.

It would not be polite for me to slight my mother without acknowledging my own kitchen disasters. At least her result was edible. Long after I had moved away from home and had children of my own, I decided to test my own baking abilities. The rest of my family was out of the house for the afternoon, and I decided to make a double batch of chocolate chip cookies to surprise them when they returned.

Paying careful attention to the recipe, I assembled what I thought was the best batch of chocolate chip cookie dough the world had ever seen. After loading up the first cookie sheet and tossing it in the oven, I popped a small sample chunk of dough into my mouth. And promptly sent it flying across the room. Instead of two cups of white sugar, I had accidentally used two cups of *salt*. The two may look alike, but they definitely don't taste alike.

Mom missed one small ingredient, and her carrot cake went from world class to something you would only serve to close relatives and pets. My cookie dough looked good and smelled good, but was worthless because I made one bad substitution. Have you ever left out one small but key ingredient to your success, and settled for results that are far below your potential? Have you ever compromised your efforts, and wound up with a bad taste in your mouth, even though you still looked good and smelled good?

"I took a few shortcuts on the foundation. No one will ever notice."

For a triathlon, each competitor must complete a 1.5 km swim, 40 km of cycling and a 10 km run. Would an athlete get the prize if he decided only to compete in two of the three legs? No, that's leaving out the baking powder.

Would he get the prize if he cheated by taking a boat instead of swimming, or taking the bus instead of running? No, that's using two cups of salt instead of two cups of sugar.

What does it mean to *"do everything"*? It doesn't mean cheating or taking shortcuts. It doesn't mean doing everything by your self. It means giving your full effort and winning with integrity, both as an individual and as part of a team. It means exhausting every legal, moral and ethical possibility, to get the prize. Never compromise the price of success. If you want to get the prize, you have to do everything. Do everything:

- With specific intent
- Even when you don't feel like it
- Even when you think you can't

Do Everything With Specific Intent

> *"It is not enough to be busy. So are the ants. The question is: what are we busy about?" – Henry David Thoreau*

Everyone today seems to be "busy". Wherever I go, people tell me how they rarely have time for the important things in life. When I ask what is keeping them so busy, I often hear about their bowling league, their son or daughter's soccer practices, their favorite television shows, and the candle party down the street. I once invited a struggling consultant to a meeting that could have led to significant business opportunities, but he declined because he wanted to watch a televised soccer game instead!

Certain friends of mine like to complain about their money woes, yet they still have season's tickets for the local hockey team, play darts every Tuesday, and may usually be found parked in front of their big screen TV. What's wrong with this picture? How can you comfortably go out to play softball and eat chicken wings when you haven't saved enough money for braces for your children?

I admit that I used to play hockey or softball four nights per week, depending on the season. I even played in a darts league for a year, until I realized that I was spending more time and money on my recreation than on things that were really important. I sold or gave away my equipment, and officially retired from organized sports and leisure activities until I became financially independent. After all, which is more important: my responsibility to my family, or my personal leisure?

Every evening, my wife and I share the duties for preparing dinner, while our children are responsible for cleaning up after the meal. Sometimes I'll sneak back into the kitchen after dinner, and find that some of our children are missing. When I track them down and ask why they are playing in their room rather than helping wash the dishes, the response is usually, "Umm...I don't know."

Whatever you are doing, ask yourself what would happen if someone snuck up behind you and asked why you are doing it. Would you feel comfortable in giving them the answer, or would you be caught saying, "Umm...I don't know," like my children sometimes are? Will the things you are doing get you closer to where you want to be? Will they improve your life, will they keep you where you are, or will they drag you a few steps back?

Make a point of always knowing why you do what you do. Choose the high road and do everything you can to get you closer to the person you were meant to become. Drop all activities that keep you from getting there. Make every moment count. Live a life of purpose. The days that you have a valid answer for the question, "Why am I doing this?" are the days that will propel you forward to a life of significance.

How do you know what activities should command your attention? Simply look at where you are and where you want to be, and ask yourself, "What is the next right thing to do to get me where I want to be?" Sometimes the next right thing is a major event, sometimes it might be to brush your teeth and go to bed. Either way, by always doing the next right thing, you keep yourself on track and never lose focus.

Ask yourself...

What is the next right thing I must do to get me closer to my goal?

Do Everything Even When You Don't Feel Like It

"There is no victory at bargain basement prices." – Dwight D. Eisenhower

When I was five years old, my mother decided that I should learn to play the piano. I had always enjoyed listening to music, and thought that it would be a great idea to learn to play. I had seen people playing piano before; it looked like it was easy and a lot of fun. I thought that I could just sit down and play the piano like a professional without any effort. She never mentioned that I would have to devote hours to practicing the basics and developing my skills.

I remember being dragged down the street, in tears, to go and visit Miss Burniston, my piano teacher. Each session was probably only fifteen or twenty minutes long, but it seemed to go on for hours. I didn't want to go through the effort to become a good piano player; I just wanted the results. After a few weeks of this torture, my mother and I finally gave up. I never learned to play the piano.

When I started playing hockey, I encountered the same obstacles. I had seen hockey players on television streaking up and down the ice, stick handling around the opposing players and shooting the puck with ease. That looks easy enough, I thought. I should be able to just step out on the ice and dazzle and amaze everyone with my hockey playing ability. Was I ever in for a surprise.

I wasn't a very good skater at first. Falling on the ice sometimes hurt, both mentally and physically. The other team, who always seemed to be much bigger and stronger, slammed me into the boards whenever I got the puck. Every Saturday morning, we practiced on an outdoor rink until we were frozen solid. I remember crying all the way home as my toes slowly and painfully warmed up in the car. It was almost as fun as the piano lessons.

But I knew what kind of hockey player I wanted to be. Unless I did everything my coaches told me to do, that dream would never be a reality. So I did everything, whether I liked doing it or not. I didn't have the talent to make it to the NHL, but I did become an above average goaltender. If I had done everything my piano teacher recommended, just as I did everything my hockey coaches required, I'd probably be an excellent piano player today. I have no one to blame but myself.

With hockey, I focused on the long-term results instead of the effort it took to get there. With piano lessons, I only saw the effort. How often do we lose sight of the long-term rewards and see only the short-term effort? Focus only on the short-term effort and the discomfort of getting to where you want to be, and you will likely quit. Keep in mind the desired results and focus on the feelings you will experience when you get there, and it will be much easier to persist. Keep your mind on the prize.

Ask yourself...

What keys to my success am I avoiding because I don't like doing them?

Do Everything Even When You Think You Can't

"If we did all the things we are capable of doing, we would literally astonish ourselves." – Thomas Edison

She used just a few simple words, but they have stayed with me for more than 20 years. Mrs. MacDonald was teaching me to swim one Sunday afternoon. Pointing to the deep end of the pool, she told me to try an underwater somersault. I wasn't a strong swimmer, and never really enjoyed my time in the water, so one of the last things I wanted to do was a somersault.

Even though it was out of my comfort zone, it somehow seemed possible, so I gave it a try. After two or three clumsy forward somersaults, she asked me to try a *backward* somersault. Well, I knew for sure that I wasn't able to do that. I would get water up my nose and drown in an instant. I was scared to even try. Confident in my lack of ability, I turned to her and said, "I can't." The words had barely left my mouth when she turned and sternly said, "There is no such word as *can't* around here, Larry." She refused to let me leave the pool until I at least attempted a backward somersault.

Looking up to the ceiling, I pushed away from the side and drifted toward the center of the pool. Bringing my knees up to my chest, I leaned back in the water. With arms and legs flailing, I awkwardly spun around and popped my head through the surface. I really *could* do a backward somersault! It wasn't pretty, it wasn't comfortable, but I did something that I thought was impossible for me to do. Mrs. MacDonald pushed me through that barrier and encouraged me to do everything, even when I didn't think I could.

Years ago, in one of my recreational hockey leagues, each team shared a wide range of talent. Some of the players had played in semi-pro leagues, while others could barely skate. Gord was a very selfish player who was more interested in his personal statistics than the welfare of our team. Even if it put him out of position, Gord always skated toward the weaker players on the other team, looking for an easy scoring opportunity. He limited his efforts to what was comfortable, and avoided the players who were tough to play against.

The rest of our team faced the most talented players on the other team, whether we felt that we could beat them or not. By playing against tough opposition and fighting the odds all year, we became good enough to handle any opponent. Gord got a lot of points during the regular season by taking shortcuts, but he was virtually useless to our team in the playoffs, since he could only play well against the weak players.

You may not succeed in your first attempt to do everything, but with each effort you grow and build your ability and endurance. Gord did the things that he knew were possible, and not a fraction more. He didn't do everything required to be truly successful. The rest of us ignored the odds, attempted the impossible, improved with each game, and won the league championship. Are you willing to forego immediate success to go for the bigger prize? Are you willing to set your opinions aside and go for the impossible?

Ask yourself...

What keys to my success am I avoiding because I think I can't do them?

Do Everything

If you decide to adopt a diet plan but don't follow it to the letter, can you honestly look back and say that the diet plan doesn't work? If you start a new business and only follow seven of the eight steps that you need to become successful, can you blame the business plan for your lack of results? Until you do everything, you have no right to doubt your ability to succeed.

On the way to getting the prize, some things may seem impossible. Some may require an extreme amount of focus, and some may just be painful. When doing everything seems too difficult, just make yourself a double batch of chocolate chip cookies with salt instead of sugar. Take a bite, and get a taste of what it's like when you don't do everything. Then make another batch with the proper ingredients, and get a taste of the prize. Which would you prefer?

"There is only one way to succeed in anything and that is to give everything. I do and I demand that my players do...I firmly believe that any man's finest hour, the greatest fulfillment of all he holds dear, is that moment when he has worked his heart out in a good cause and lies exhausted on the field of battle – victorious."
– Vince Lombardi

Chapter 6
Work At It With All Your Heart

Whatever you do, work at it with all your heart, as working for the Lord, not for men, since you know that you will receive an inheritance from the Lord as a reward... – Colossians 3:23-24

Lizbeth was the best babysitter our children ever had. Her sister, Diana, was also one of their favorites. Often we had just enough time to pick Lizbeth up, bring her back to our house and dash back out the door with the dinner dishes still on the table, and the house a mess. Even so, we always returned to clean dishes and a spotless kitchen. All of the toys were put away and our shoes were lined up neatly by the front door.

Lizbeth and her family eventually moved away, and we were forced to find other babysitters. Some left the house messier than it was when they arrived. One spent the night on the telephone, including three long distance calls that showed up on our next month's bill. Another spent the entire time playing on our computer instead of watching the children. Only one of the new sitters was even close to Lizbeth's quality.

We never asked Lizbeth to wash the dishes or straighten up the house. She simply saw a need and filled it. Our house was always cleaner on our return than it was when we departed. On some occasions, we begged her to leave dishes for us to wash, just so we wouldn't feel so guilty. Lizbeth was a successful babysitter, and will be successful at whatever she does, simply because she works at it with all her heart.

Remember Barth, my statics teacher? He taught with all his heart. That same year, our physics professor did not. The textbook was too heavy for him to carry, so he tore out only the required pages to bring to class. He sat in his chair while writing on the blackboard, because it was too much effort to stand up. He showed no interest in the material, and seemed much more concerned about dismissing us ahead of schedule so he could get an early lunch.

A large number of us developed the same heartless attitude toward the material, and reaped the rewards of that attitude. Physics was my best subject in high school, but I failed it that year. Now, I am not blaming our physics professor for my lack of success. I had the option to choose a better attitude, and simply didn't. But I learned that the attitude you bring to your work might be contagious. Who is watching and learning from your work ethic?

Have you ever worked at something with all your heart? Do you remember how fulfilled you felt after giving that project all that you had to give? How would you like to look back on every day of your life knowing that you gave your full effort to your calling? Focus on these three keys:

- Work at your vocation
- Work hard
- Work smart

Work At Your Vocation

> *"If a man is called to be a street sweeper, he should sweep streets even as Michelangelo painted, or Beethoven composed music, or Shakespeare wrote poetry. He should sweep streets so well that all the host of heaven and earth will pause to say, here lived a great street sweeper who did his job well." – Martin Luther King*

Roughly 20 years ago, when people still believed in job security, my hockey teammate Morris held a safe, secure government job. For fifteen years he had built up a healthy pension, extra vacation time and great benefits. His job provided him with a comfortable lifestyle, but it was not what he was called to do with his life. After fifteen years, Morris realized that he was meant to be a welder.

When he told his friends and coworkers that he was quitting his job, most of them said he was crazy. No one in their right mind would give up that kind of money, security and benefits. Rather than congratulate him on leaving his comfort zone and pursuing his vocation, they did everything possible to discourage him. Thankfully, Morris didn't pay attention to their advice. He started his own welding shop and never looked back.

Why did everyone discourage Morris from pursuing his vocation? By identifying his passion and pursuing it, he reminded many of them that they had never pursued their true calling either. They had settled for whatever job was available, clung to their secure paycheck, and stuck with things that were familiar and simple. They had found their comfort zone, and now Morris was making them uncomfortable.

Have you ever met someone who loves what they do? Sadly, they are in the minority. Morris sacrificed his short-term security to gain the long-term satisfaction of working at his vocation. He knew that life is too short to work at something you don't enjoy, or something that you haven't been called to do. What work would inspire you to get up in the morning without an alarm clock? What work would you consider a pleasure rather than a necessary evil?

Are you working at your vocation today? Is there anything in your life that you really should be doing, but aren't? Have you missed becoming the person you were meant to be because you decided to play it safe, or are you already well on your way? Are you merely making a living, or are you making a life?

Ask yourself...

What is my vocation?

What should I be doing to realize it?

Work Hard

"We will receive not what we idly wish for but what we justly earn. Our rewards will always be in exact proportion to our service." – Earl Nightingale

Dave was the shortest and skinniest player on our hockey team. He was not a very good skater, and didn't handle the puck with much skill. But he worked harder than anyone else on the ice. Joe was a naturally gifted athlete who could have turned professional in several sports. He was probably more talented than anyone else on our team. But Joe never worked hard. Sometimes I wondered why he even bothered to show up.

Even though Joe could have skated circles around everyone in the league, Dave regularly outperformed him. By sheer hard work, Dave created more opportunities for himself and the team than Joe ever did. He drove the other teams crazy, because he was relentless in keeping them off balance and chasing down the puck. No one could watch Dave perform and say that he was giving a half-hearted effort.

Dave compensated for his lack of natural ability by working harder than anyone else on the team. If Joe had applied the same effort to his game, he would have had no trouble becoming a professional hockey player. Look at some of the great athletes of our era. Michael Jordan, Wayne Gretzky and Tiger Woods were all blessed with talent, but they also worked harder than the average player to become the best at their sport.

Remember Tony and John from the die shop? Tony, even though he was greatly underpaid, worked hard at each project to get it done correctly and on time. He developed the habit of hard work long before he was rewarded for it. John never worked hard, and made it known that he wouldn't work hard until he got a raise. Who would you rather have as an employee? After he was fired, John realized that the reward comes after hard work, not before.

Like John, are you holding back from hard work because your average attempts haven't been rewarded? Large rewards require large efforts. Are you afraid that you might not have the talent to produce the desired results? Dave proved that abundant effort compensates for sparse talent. In the long run, you will be rewarded according to your work habits. Are you working as hard as you can?

Ask yourself...

What do I need to work hard at?

How hard can I work at it?

Work Smart

> *"The great difference between those who succeed and those who fail does not consist in the amount of work done by each but in the amount of intelligent work." – Og Mandino*

There is no point in working hard if you don't also work smart. If you start up your car, shift it into neutral and hold the gas pedal to the floor, your engine is working at its vocation. Your engine is working hard. But is it working smart? Until your vehicle is put in gear, and that hard work is applied to a specific purpose, it isn't working smart. It is only running out of gas.

Are you working harder than you need to work? Many years ago, I was helping to load some parts onto an assembly line. The parts bin sat two or three steps away, so I had to walk back and forth every few seconds to get more. Seeing that I wasn't working smart, the supervisor moved the bin closer to the assembly line so I could do all of my work from one location. That small adjustment saved hours of time and effort.

Are you working at something other than your strengths? I am forever grateful to my wife and children for letting me work smart. As a family, we realized that everyone in our house could wash dishes, but only I could write this book. Instead of expecting me to wash my share of the dishes, they encouraged me to channel my efforts into writing. What tasks can you delegate so you can focus on your strengths?

Are you devaluing your time? For example, a friend of mine spends hours every month driving from store to store to save pennies on his household goods. Why not pay a small premium for convenience and spend those hours on something more productive? Are you focusing your time on pursuits that will give you the best return for your investment? Where and how would you invest your time to get the most out of every day?

Are you using all available resources? Are there tools available to simplify your work? Are there people more experienced and successful than you who have wisdom to offer? Are there systems in place that you can take advantage of? Time is our most precious, non-renewable resource. Whether we like it or not, our time is limited. Would you rather be busy, or productive?

Ask yourself...

What activities will make the best use of my unique talents?

What other activities can I delegate, so I can concentrate on my unique talents?

How can I simplify my efforts to get better results?

Work At It With All Your Heart

When I was studying industrial design in college, we usually worked on three or four projects at a time, each for a different subject. Sometimes we stayed up all night working on the last minute details of one project, and started nodding off in our class the next day. One of our professors, Bob, yelled at us when we tried to prop ourselves up to stay awake during his class. He always said, "Be vertical or horizontal, but don't hover somewhere in between!"

Bob gave us permission to put our heads down on our desks and catch a quick nap. He wanted us to work at everything with all our heart. He would rather have us sleep through his class and catch up with him later, than give it a half-hearted effort. Everything you do should be worthy of all your heart, or why bother doing it? Are you hovering somewhere between vertical and horizontal? Do you work at whatever you do with all your heart?

"No matter how small and unimportant what we are doing may seem, if we do it well, it may soon become the step that will lead us to better things." – Channing Pollock

Chapter 7
Sharpen

As iron sharpens iron, so one man sharpens another. – Proverbs 27:17

Who sharpens you? You were born helpless, without the skills and knowledge to survive on your own. Someone clothed you, sheltered you, fed you and protected you from all kinds of harm. Someone taught you how to walk, how to talk and how to feed yourself. Everything you have achieved has been with someone else's assistance. You would not have made it this far in life unless a lot of people decided to help you.

I shudder whenever I walk into a bookstore and see that they have a "self help" section. When I hear someone mention that they know or are a "self made" man or woman, I cringe. There is no such thing as self help. There is no such thing as a self made man or a self made woman. Ask anyone who is truly successful and they will give credit to a number of people and events that spurred them on to success.

Remember Jamie and his grade three teacher? Mrs. Larin was his mentor. She challenged him to rise above the expectations of his friends. She shared the wisdom of choosing positive relationships, and encouraged him to work toward his new life with all his heart. While friends tend to accept you for who you are, mentors will challenge and assist you to become the person you were meant to be. Friends may leave you dull; mentors will sharpen you. Dare to have mentors as well as friends!

As a young softball player, I was very skinny and wasn't able to hit the ball very far. My strength was hitting line drives that dropped in front of or between the outfielders. It was very rare for me to hit the ball beyond an outfielder, but one August evening I sent the ball sailing over the left fielder's head, astonishing everyone on the team, including myself. They all cheered and patted me on the back, except our shortstop Jim.

As we walked back onto the field, he tapped me on the shoulder and simply said, "Nice hit, but that's not your swing." He knew that I would go up for my next at bat and try to clobber the ball again. In the process, I would ignore my strengths and develop bad swing habits. The rest of the team simply shared my joy, but Jim knew that he had to burst my bubble for me to be a better player. I am very thankful that he did.

Who coaches you in your spiritual life? Who sharpens your relationships? Who guides your business life? Who is your financial mentor? Stop listening to the people who have nothing but opinions; seek advice only from people who are already successful in each area. Swallow your pride if you have to. Ask them the right questions, and be ready to accept and apply the right answers. The right mentors will offer you these three keys:

- Challenge
- Wisdom
- Encouragement

Challenge

> *"Our chief want in life is somebody who will make us do what we can." – Ralph Waldo Emerson*

This book is the result of a challenge. Over the last five years, I have enjoyed dozens of personal development books, hundreds of audios and dozens of seminars. I have developed relationships with successful people from all walks of life. I have gleaned wisdom from many sources, and had a dream of one day compiling that wisdom into a "greatest hits" collection, so other people could share and apply it for their own success.

Last year, I sat in a room with about 20 other people who were considering consulting as a career option. Donna was our facilitator that day, and she asked each of us to share our background, our passions, and what we would like to accomplish in the future. When I mentioned that I would like to write a book after I became "successful" in four or five years, she stopped, stared at me and bluntly said, "Why aren't you writing it *now?*"

Donna made me realize that the principles in this book are proven, right and true whether I apply them or not, and they need to be known today. What purpose was I serving by holding back? By putting these principles in writing, she also challenged me to apply them in my own life and strive to be an example for others. With that one question she became a mentor to me, and prodded me closer to getting the prize.

As a young goaltender, I practiced once a week with a men's hockey team that my father coached. After four years of practice and playing in other leagues, I improved my skills to the point where I became part of Dad's team as a back-up goalie. Phil, our number one goalie, was a much better player than I was. He didn't have to, but he welcomed me to the team and gladly shared the playing time with me.

Phil and I never talked about it, but we had an understanding. He and the team allowed me to play in his place, as long as I gave an equal or better effort than he would give to the team. As an added bonus, Jim the shortstop was also the captain of our hockey team. Every week, both Jim and Phil challenged me to give my best. Between the two of them, they raised my game to new levels. With Phil's blessing, I eventually replaced him as our full time goalie.

Your mentors will challenge you to look beyond today's failures and successes, and to strive for your true potential. Your mentors will stretch you beyond the limits of your personal confidence. Your mentors will make you feel uncomfortable. If your mentors are really effective, you may even dislike them. But you will thank them later for pushing you to where you would not go on your own. You will thank them for getting you closer to the prize.

Ask yourself...

Who challenges me to reach my full potential?

How can I spend more time with them?

Where will I find more people like them?

Wisdom

> *Wisdom is supreme; therefore get wisdom. Though it cost all you have, get understanding.*
> *– Proverbs 4:7*

If you want to have a fruitful marriage, should you take guidance from someone who has been happily married for many years, or someone who is going through their third divorce? If you want financial advice, should you ask someone who is financially independent or someone who lives paycheck to paycheck? If you want to discover the merits of a business idea, should you direct your concerns to someone who is successful in that business or someone who has failed?

In my quest to climb the corporate ladder, I devoted several months to studying all of the theory behind production and inventory management, and earned some initials after my name to prove it. But all of that theory had never seen any practical application. One of my superiors had very little formal education, but had years of hands on experience. The wisdom I gained from his mentorship quickly outweighed the months of theory that I had endured.

It makes sense to seek mentorship from someone who is already successful. Opinions are like armpits – everybody has a couple, and sometimes they stink. Find mentors who have proven results rather than just opinions. Value the practical over theory. You will discover that people who are truly successful, and who are secure with their success, are eager to help you and others achieve. Could it be because someone else has done the same for them?

Have you ever read *How to Win Friends and Influence People,* by Dale Carnegie? Since its first publication in 1937, it has helped millions of readers improve their people skills. After a few hours of reading, you may learn and apply some of its principles and realize dramatic results in your personal and professional life. In just a few hours, you will have gleaned the distilled wisdom of 15 years of research, from a man who died in 1955.

For an investment of just a few hours and a few dollars, you may benefit from fifteen years of someone else's labor and experience. What a bargain! You can learn in one day what another person took years to discover. By choosing the right books, you are able to condense years of struggle, trial and error, frustration and victory into a few short hours. The wisdom of ages is waiting for you; it is only the turn of a page away.

You are standing at the edge of a minefield, with your dreams and goals on the other side. The only way to reach them is to cross the field. You have a few options: you may cross the field blindly, at your chosen pace, hoping to miss the mines along the way. You may use a map drawn up by someone who hasn't crossed the field, but who *thinks* they know where the mines are. Or you may follow in the footprints of someone who has already made it across. Make the wise choice.

Ask yourself...

Who has the wisdom I need to reach my full potential?

How can I spend more time with them?

Where will I find more people like them?

Encouragement

> *"In everyone's life, at some time, our inner fire goes out. It is then burst into flames by an encounter with another human being. We should all be thankful for those people who rekindle the inner spirit." – Albert Schweitzer*

It was the middle of winter, and our physical education teacher still made us run laps outside. Snow covered the track, but all of the driveways and parking lots had been cleared, so we ran around the school instead. In shorts and t-shirts, we had to circle the building four times before going back inside to warm up. Each time around the school must have been a quarter of a mile, and after three laps we were getting tired. The pace had slowed to little more than a brisk walk.

Just then Mr. Hunt, one of our English teachers, stepped outside from the weight room. Here was a 64-year-old grandfather, in better physical shape than some of us teenagers, making his way across the parking lot in bright spandex pants. He shouted his support, and the pace picked up. He encouraged us with his words, and also with his example. He wasn't an out of shape spectator who was shouting commands. He was a fellow participant who was cheering us on.

While honing my public speaking skills, I practiced giving short presentations with a local club. A number of the members were excellent speakers, and I looked forward to receiving their evaluation forms after each of my speeches. They pulled me out of my comfort zone, challenged me to improve in certain areas and offered their wisdom about how to make those improvements. It wasn't always comfortable for me, but I knew it was what I needed to realize my dream of being a professional speaker.

Their evaluations worked because they always wrapped them up with a word of encouragement. They helped me keep my focus on the prize, rather than the effort it took to reach it. Could you imagine receiving a challenge to improve, being pointed in the direction of the resources, then being abandoned with no positive reinforcement? Mentors who have been where you want to go are the best encouragers, because they know that it can be done.

For example, mention to an author that you want to be an author one day, and the ones worth following will be full of encouragement and insight. Mention that dream to your close relatives, friends and associates who have never written a book before, and many of them will try to beat the dream out of you with their opinions. Who would you rather listen to? Who do you think I listened to? Remember to look for mentors, not *tormentors.*

Ask yourself...

Who encourages me to reach my full potential?

How can I spend more time with them?

Where will I find more people like them?

Sharpen

I still remember bringing home a report card in grade four with straight A's and a note from Mrs. Tomlinson, "Larry is starting to get a little lazy." She was right, but I was upset. I was hoping to ride those straight A's from grade four all the way through high school. Sadly, I never did break away from that habit of doing minimal schoolwork, and my grades eventually suffered. If I had listened in grade four, I might have had an easier time later on in school.

Mentors offer you challenge, wisdom and encouragement, but you are the one who must put them to good use. When Jim interrupted my home run celebration, I had the option of ignoring him and trying to swing for the fences every time. When Donna challenged me to start writing, I could have procrastinated. I could have shunned my boss's wisdom and floundered in my new job. As long as you are willing to settle for less than your best, mentorship is optional.

Your mentors are your insurance policy against complacency and mediocrity. Remember, there is no such thing as a self-made man or woman. There are resources out there to challenge you. The wisdom you need is available. There are people out there who are interested in your success, who will encourage you to become all that you were meant to be. Who sharpens you?

"A hundred times every day I remind myself that my inner and outer life depend on the labors of other men, living and dead, and that I must exert myself in order to give in the same measure as I have received and am still receiving." – Albert Einstein

Chapter 8
Sow Generously

> *Remember this: Whoever sows sparingly will reap sparingly, and whoever sows generously will also reap generously.*
> *– 2 Corinthians 9:6*

I used to coordinate the staff for a small personnel agency. A customer of ours called one day, looking for a truck driver to start at five o'clock the next morning. I called several people, and none of them were interested. When I spoke with Desmond, he wasn't terribly enthusiastic about it either, but he knew that I was desperate. He promised to show up the next morning if I needed him, as long as I had exhausted all other possibilities first.

After phoning everyone else on my list, Desmond was my only hope. I called him back and begged him to help me, at least for one day. He agreed to show up at our customer's office as a favor to me. I had only met him a few days before, and had no idea how reliable he would be. Not wanting to take any chances, I got up early the following morning and went to make sure that our customer had a driver that day.

When we met in the parking lot at ten minutes to five, Desmond realized that I was willing to put forth an extra effort to get the job done, and I realized that he had the integrity to follow through on his promises. We both planted a seed that morning that led to a long-term friendship. If you want to develop a trusting relationship, you have to prove yourself worthy of trust. In other words, if you want to reap trust, you must first sow trust. Desmond is now a mentor to me, and to my oldest son.

Smart business people are always looking for opportunities to network. But at every event I attend, there seems to be at least one person with strictly selfish motives. Last year, I sat with a networking group of unemployed executives.

One participant eagerly handed out his resume and asked us all for potential employment leads. To my amazement, though, he never took down anyone else's information with the hopes of helping them in return. Without hesitation, I threw his resume in the garbage.

At another networking session, one member of our table dominated the conversation and pestered us for contacts, strictly so he could solicit his own business. It was obvious that he wasn't looking for an exchange; he was only interested in what we could do for him. He got very little cooperation from the rest of the table, because he violated what I believe is a vital rule of networking: never ask other people for help unless you truly are willing to help them first.

I know what you may be thinking. Doesn't that go against the principle of asking, the principle that we just read about in Chapter 3? No, it doesn't! When an opportunity arises, make sure you ask for it. But remember also to do your homework and offer something in exchange whenever possible. If you want to reap assistance through networking, be prepared to sow some of your own networking assistance first. Sowing comes before reaping.

It just makes sense. We reap what we sow. If you want good things to happen for you, you must help good things happen for others. If you want to have more money and time flexibility tomorrow, you need to invest money and time today. If you want people to treat you with respect, you need to treat yourself and others with respect. How can we sow to make sure we reap the maximum reward? Remember to:

- Sow wisely
- Sow willingly
- Sow selflessly

Sow Wisely

> *"There would be no advantage to be gained by sowing a field of wheat if the harvest did not return more than was sown." – Napoleon Hill*

Where do you sow your time, money, and talents? Do you sow where you know there will be a harvest? While writing this chapter, I had a nightmare that woke me up in a cold sweat. In my dream, I was playing video pinball. Sitting beside me was one of my mentors, a multi-millionaire entrepreneur. He was sharing his wisdom about business, life and success, but I was so focused on my game that I never heard a word.

My dream became a nightmare when I suddenly realized that I had been ignoring him for several minutes. He had been sowing seeds of wisdom where there was no chance of a harvest, and he was not going to continue. He was going to take those seeds and sow them where someone would listen to them, apply them, and yield a harvest. I had lost the mentorship of a multi-millionaire for the sake of a silly pinball game!

That thought jolted me awake, and kept me awake for a long time. I no longer play that pinball game, even when I'm alone. That nightmare taught me to appreciate when someone sows some seeds my way, and to do my best to yield a bountiful harvest. I also learned to consider where I am sowing *my* resources, and to make sure that my time, money, and talents are sown into relationships and activities that will yield a full harvest.

Every day, we are given 24 hours to sow. When the average American spends four of those hours watching television, what is the harvest? How are you sowing your time? What will your harvest be? Where could your time be better spent? Make sure you sow the appropriate amount of time for whatever you want to reap. Once today is gone, it is gone forever. Will the time you sow give you the harvest you are looking for?

How are you sowing your money? What will be your harvest? My favorite charity is run completely by volunteers. One hundred percent of donations go directly to help children and cottage industries in underdeveloped countries. I consider that sowing wisely, since every penny goes toward the harvest. Where does your money go? Are you making every dollar count toward a worthwhile harvest, or is your income literally "disposable"?

How are you sowing your talents? Are you sowing them at all? What will be your harvest? A friend of mine is a gifted artist, but she never used to show anyone her work. With the encouragement of her friends, she now knows that her talent is wasted unless it is sown for others to appreciate. Why hide your talents, when someone could benefit from them? Whenever you sow time, money or talents, consider the harvest.

Ask yourself...

What is the best way to sow my time?

What is the best way to sow my money?

What is the best way to sow my talents?

What is the expected harvest?

Sow Willingly

Each man should give what he has decided in his heart to give, not reluctantly or under compulsion, for God loves a cheerful giver. – 2 Corinthians 9:7

My youngest son loves to sing in the bathroom. When the door is closed and no one else is in sight, he serenades the rest of the house at the top of his lungs. When we ask him to sing outside the bathroom, he usually refuses. He is not comfortable when he sings alone in front of other people, and it shows. His bathroom music is always much better, simply because he sings willingly.

I enjoy watching live musical performances, where musicians sow their talent and energy to reap the applause of an approving audience. Most of the concerts I've attended have been great experiences, but once or twice I have been disappointed. Strangely, it had more to do with the musician's attitude than ability. Two years ago, I went to see a friend's band perform. Their lead guitar player was extremely talented, but he looked like he didn't want to be there.

He never smiled, never made eye contact with the audience, and never showed any passion for the music. He played the guitar well, but since he didn't appear to be sowing his talents willingly, he lost our appreciation. The lead singer was a less talented musician, but we could tell that she was gladly giving her best effort to entertain us. By sowing her talents willingly, she won over the audience, and saved the show.

When I asked Desmond to drive a truck at five o'clock in the morning, I knew that it was something that he didn't want to do. Yet he sowed his time and effort willingly, not because he enjoyed doing it, but because he knew that I needed his help. If he had grumbled through the whole ordeal, and let me know that he really didn't want to be there, we never would have developed a friendship.

People can tell whether you are sowing willingly, or against your will. Sowing willingly improves the seed. It makes others more receptive and willing to return a harvest. Sowing willingly attracts other people who will help you sow. Sowing willingly attracts other opportunities to sow, and to reap. Are you sowing your time, money and talents willingly?

Ask yourself...

Where do I not sow willingly?

How can I change it for the better?

Sow Selflessly

> *"The true meaning of life is to plant trees, under whose shade you do not expect to sit." – Nelson Henderson*

My friend John and I were taking part in a workshop that challenged us to define some of our dreams. We each filled out a worksheet, broke off into pairs and shared answers with our assigned partner. He shared some amazing dreams of owning his own helicopter, golfing all over the world and traveling to major sporting events. But what impressed me most was his attitude about giving.

The question read, "If money were not an issue, I would give _______." While most of us filled in the blank with a measure of money, time or talents, John simply wrote the word, "anonymously". I learned a lot about John that day, and gained a tremendous amount of respect for him. John was willing to quietly sow where someone else could benefit, without any fanfare or personal gain.

When I was in my early teens, my parents and I visited Miss Williams every week. She had no surviving relatives, and most of her friends had passed away. She was confined to a wheelchair, but she loved to swim. The pool where Mrs. MacDonald worked had special wheelchair access, so we took Miss Williams there for a few hours every weekend. She swam laps in the shallow end, while Mrs. MacDonald encouraged me to do somersaults in the deep end.

After our swim, we took Miss Williams home and visited for a while. It was obvious that she was lonely and enjoyed our company. I would like to say that I visited strictly because it meant so much to her, but I am ashamed to admit that I had ulterior motives. I knew that her brother, who had passed away a few years earlier, had an extensive rock collection in the basement. I was hoping that she would one day clean out the basement, and pass the collection on to me.

It wasn't right for me to expect a personal harvest from sowing time with Miss Williams. Our visiting time should have been for her benefit alone. As weeks turned into months, and months turned into years, my interest waned. I stopped going to see Miss Williams, and I never did get my hands on that rock collection. I didn't deserve it. When sowing your time, money and talents, the harvest doesn't have to be all yours.

Miss Williams could probably tell that I wasn't there for the right reasons. Just as I sniffed out the two selfish networkers, others can sense when you are sowing only for personal gain. Remember that we reap what we sow. Are you sowing strictly for your own harvest, or are you sowing for the benefit of others?

Ask yourself...

How have I benefited from someone else's selfless sowing?

How could I sow selflessly?

Sow Generously

Every day we are sowing seeds. Sometimes we see the harvest, sometimes we don't. Either way, we reap what we sow. Vince was one of my friends in high school. After we graduated, several of us still gathered every few weeks for a social evening. We lived close together, so each one of us took turns driving to different events. No one seemed to mind sharing the responsibility, except Vince.

When it was his first turn to drive, Vince had three of us as passengers. At the end of the evening, he dropped all three of us off at a mutual friend's house. As we were getting out of the car, he held his hand out and demanded gas money. As only teenage boys can do, we verbally abused him for being so cheap, and promptly left him empty-handed. We never invited Vince to another event.

By sowing ill will among his friends, Vince reaped a harvest of ill will. By sowing his time and talents when I was in need, Desmond earned my immediate respect. He eventually reaped the use of my time and talents in return. What would you like to reap in your spiritual life, relationships, business life and finances? Sow sparingly, and you will reap sparingly. Sow generously, and you will reap generously. What are you willing to sow?

"Sow an act, and you reap a habit. Sow a habit and you reap a character. Sow a character, and you reap a destiny."
– Charles Reade

Chapter 9

Let Your Light Shine

"You are the light of the world. A city on a hill cannot be hidden. Neither do people light a lamp and put it under a bowl. Instead they put it on its stand, and it gives light to everyone in the house. In the same way, let your light shine before men, that they may see your good deeds and praise your Father in heaven." – Matthew 5:14-16

Many years ago, some friends and I invented the dangerous (and thankfully, short-lived) sport of Flashlight Catch. Our softball team had traveled over 100 miles to a weekend tournament. Some of our less rugged players checked in to a motel, but the rest of us stayed at a campsite a few miles from town. We pulled in to the secluded campground on Friday evening, and pitched our tents at the crest of a hill, beside a large open field.

We quickly built a campfire, and sat around swapping stories of games gone by. Before long, a few of us became restless. Someone suggested that we play catch, but with overcast skies, no lights around for miles, and the campfire on the other side of the hill, the field beside us was completely dark. "No problem," Dave said. He mounted the hill with his lawn chair, faced it toward the field, and grabbed a large flashlight.

Bob and I ran out into the field with our gloves and a ball, and lined up about sixty feet apart. Starting slowly, we tossed the ball back and forth while "Dave the Light Man" tracked it with the beam of his flashlight. Every time that we completed a throw, our confidence grew. Dave let his light shine as we threw harder and faster, until we were finally firing the ball back and forth at top speed.

Then, disaster struck. Dave briefly got distracted from his light shining duties. Bob didn't notice, and sent the ball screaming into the darkness. I now had an invisible, leather-bound missile hurtling toward me at 80 miles per hour. What happened next must have looked like a prison break. Dave frantically waved the flashlight back and forth to locate the ball in midair, while I ran like a madman to get out of its way. Somehow I avoided the ball, and it sailed past me into the night. That marked the end of our game.

We played with confidence when Dave let his light shine. When he stopped letting his light shine, we quit and went to bed. Whether you like it or not, you are somebody's "Dave the Light Man". Whether you know it or not, your actions have an effect on the performance and attitude of others. Your example shines a light to guide them. There are people out there, waiting and hoping for you to light their way.

Running as to get the prize doesn't just mean putting yourself in a position to win. It also means setting a pace, an example for others to follow. How do we let our light shine for the benefit of others? As we learned in chapter seven, the principles in this book are proven, right and true. Someone has already studied them, applied them and taught them to others through their example. To let your light shine, take these principles for yourself and:

- Study them
- Apply them
- Teach them through example

Study

> *"Get over the idea that only children should spend their time in study. Be a student so long as you still have something to learn, and this will mean all your life."*
> *– Henry L. Doherty*

Jim the shortstop once invited another Dave to play with us at a softball tournament. Jim described him simply as "a student of the game". At first I wasn't sure what Jim meant, but it soon became quite obvious. Before every game, Dave grabbed his bat and an old ball. He walked over to a remote area of the ballpark, and hit the ball into the fence five times. He took that time to study and refine his swing.

Dave also studied the other team throughout the game. He observed their weaknesses, strengths, and the patterns that they followed in their play. He used that knowledge to our team's advantage, reminding us what to expect from different players, encouraging us to reap the most rewards for our effort. Dave approached every game as an opportunity to learn and improve. No wonder he was one of our better players that weekend.

At the time, I didn't realize that Jim paid Dave a great compliment by calling him a student. To me, admitting that you were a student of your profession meant that you didn't know enough, that you were somehow inadequate. I would have been much more impressed if Jim told us that Dave was an "expert" softball player. How about you? Would you rather be considered a student, or an expert? Are there any areas in your life where you have become an "expert"?

My friend Mark once told me a story that opened my eyes. He was working with his mentor to solve an unusual problem. Feeling overwhelmed, Mark jokingly said to his mentor, "Well, you're the expert." His mentor quickly replied, "Mark, never call me an expert. Let me tell you what an expert is. An 'ex' is a has-been, and a 'spurt' is a drip under pressure." When I thought about it, he was right. Experts are complacent and smug. Experts know a lot about old stuff. Experts have stopped running for the prize.

Remember Barth? Even after 25 years of teaching, he chose to remain a student of his profession, refusing to consider himself an expert. That choice opened him up to the rewards of constant growth, and steady progress toward the prize. I now know why he always had a spring in his step and a sparkle in his eye. In the race of life, the prize goes to the student, not the expert. Are you a student? What have you learned today?

Ask yourself...

What are the top three things I have learned from reading this book?

Apply

"In the end we retain from our studies only that which we practically apply." – Johann Wolfgang Von Goethe

I used to play golf regularly as a teenager. Without taking any lessons, I developed improper habits in my stance, grip and swing. Those habits quickly became comfortable, even though they led to substandard results. I could have significantly improved my game with the help of a coach, but one obstacle got in the way – me. I didn't want to face the discomfort of "unlearning" those bad habits.

Remember the twins, Jane and Jeff? They both became comfortable with a set of habits. Jeff's habits led him away from the prize, while Jane's habits propelled her toward the prize. We all have developed our own comfortable habits. No doubt, some of those habits are keeping us from the prize. No doubt, we can change our habits for the better. No doubt, we don't want to go through that uncomfortable change.

Some golfers seek professional advice to improve their game. They learn how to refine their stance, grip and swing. But once they get out on the golf course, their new swing doesn't feel comfortable. As they struggle with the adjustments, they don't always see immediate, significant results. Many get discouraged and slip back into their old, comfortable habits. They never give themselves a chance to apply the things that they learned.

If your current financial situation reflects fifteen years of money management habits, is it realistic to expect a significant turnaround within fifteen *weeks*? If you gained an extra 20 pounds over the last two years, is it reasonable to expect to lose that extra weight within two weeks? Expect results from applying these principles, but don't expect them to appear overnight.

Look back at the principles you have learned. Just like adopting a new golf stance, grip or swing, applying them may not feel comfortable right away. As you struggle with the adjustments, you may not see significant short-term results. Will you get discouraged and slip back into your old habits, or will you keep your eye on the prize, and break through? Remember that the choice is yours!

Ask yourself...

How will I apply the top three things I have learned?

Teach Through Example

> *"Example is not the main thing in influencing others, it is the only thing." – Albert Schweitzer*

Every spring, our softball team met to discuss our tournament schedule for the year. Some players had young families, and warned us in advance that they couldn't commit to every tournament. One of our younger, single players snubbed them for their "lack of commitment," and encouraged our team leaders to register for as many tournaments as possible, since he and his friends planned to attend every one.

While he tried to impress us with his talk of commitment, that same player soon lost all of his credibility. Ignoring his springtime promise, he and two teammates booked a fishing trip on the same weekend as a major tournament. We needed at least ten players to participate in the tournament, and their absence dropped our roster to eight. We were so desperate for replacements that my father, who was in his sixties, had to play that weekend to keep us from losing by default.

From then on, our team had no unity. Through their example, those three players taught each of us to put ourselves ahead of the team. We didn't *consciously* decide to become selfish. Most of us didn't even recognize what was happening at the time. But whether we noticed it or not, that current of selfishness ate away at our team. The actions of those three players cast a shadow on our team that made the difference between victory and defeat.

Teaching through words is not effective unless you back up those words with consistent example. Your attitude and commitment shine a light for those around you, whether good or bad, whether you are aware of it or not, whether you like it or not. What are you teaching with your example today? Take the principles you have learned from these pages, apply them to your life, and live the example you want others to model.

Ask yourself...

Who will I teach, through my example, the top three things I have learned?

Let Your Light Shine

Just before writing this paragraph, I spoke on the telephone with Werner Barth for the first time in over 16 years. There were two reasons for me to give him a call. First, I wanted permission to mention him in this book. But, more importantly, I was 16 years late in thanking him for the effect he has had on my life. Until today, he never knew how much he influenced me by letting his light shine.

Even over the phone, he lit up the room with his enthusiasm. He has been retired from teaching for 14 years, and is still quite active physically and mentally. He told me about his hiking trip last weekend, and how he had beaten colon cancer a few years ago. He spoke with a positive attitude and appreciation for life that surpassed just about anyone I've ever known. When I grow up, I want to be just like him.

In a world of conformity, complacency and mediocrity, people like Barth are a breath of fresh air. He is constantly active, and has a positive outlook that is downright infectious. As a teacher, he taught for the love of teaching, not for status or money. He found his vocation and let his light shine. As a result, he is one of the most fulfilled people I have met. Would you like to live a life of significance? Would you like to live a life of fulfillment? Take your lamp out from under the bowl, and let your light shine.

"You are not here merely to make a living. You are here in order to enable the world to live more amply, with greater vision, with a finer spirit of hope and achievement. You are here to enrich the world, and you impoverish yourself if you forget the errand." – Woodrow T. Wilson

Epilogue

Be Transformed

> *Do not conform any longer to the pattern of this world, but be transformed by the renewing of your mind... – Romans 12:2*

A baseball on a shelf is worth a few dollars. In the hands of a major league pitcher, that same baseball is worth millions. A football on a shelf is worth a few dollars. In the hands of an NFL quarterback, that same football is worth millions. A basketball on a shelf is worth a few dollars. In the hands of a star NBA point guard, that same basketball is worth millions. This book on a shelf is worth a few dollars. What will it be worth in your hands?

That pitcher was not born with the ability to throw a 90-mile per hour fastball. That quarterback was not born with the ability to toss a 36-yard touchdown pass. That basketball player *was* born with the ability to dribble, but not with a basketball! It took years of above average effort for them to become the elite of their calling. They did not conform to the pattern of this world. Rather, they did what other people *would* not do, so they could later do what other people *could* not do.

The pattern of this world does not lead to the prize. The prize comes at a price that most people aren't willing to pay. Those three athletes spent years developing their skills. They practiced when others weren't willing to practice, sacrificed when others weren't willing to sacrifice. They faced their critics who said it couldn't be done. They renewed their mind, focused on the prize rather than the price, and pressed on.

Choose to break from the pattern of this world. Step out from the bleachers, and onto the playing field of life. Could it be a long time before you see significant results? Yes. Will it be difficult? Yes. Will it be uncomfortable?

Yes. Will you be misunderstood? Yes. Will you be discouraged? Yes. Will you stumble and fall along the way? Yes. At each hurdle, renew your mind, focus on the prize, and press on.

In a race, all the runners run, but only one gets the prize. Run in such a way as to get the prize.

"Do not go where the path may lead, go instead where there is no path and leave a trail." – Ralph Waldo Emerson

On your mark, get set...

The Race

By D.H. (Dee) Groberg

I

"Quit! Give Up! You're beaten!"
They shout at me and plead.
"There's just too much against you now.
This time you can't succeed."

And as I start to hang my head
In front of failure's face,
My downward fall is broken by
The memory of a race.

And hope refills my weakened will
As I recall that scene;
For just the thought of that short race
Rejuvenates my being.

II

A children's race--young boys, young men--
How I remember well.
Excitement, sure! But also fear;
It wasn't hard to tell.

They all lined up so full of hope
Each thought to win that race.
Or tie for first, or if not that,
At least take second place.

And fathers watched from off the side
Each cheering for his son.
And each boy hoped to show his dad
That he would be the one.

The whistle blew and off they went
Young hearts and hopes afire.
To win and be the hero there
Was each young boy's desire.

And one boy in particular
Whose dad was in the crowd
Was running near the lead and thought:
"My dad will be so proud!"

But as they speeded down the field
Across a shallow dip,
The little boy who thought to win
Lost his step and slipped.

Trying hard to catch himself
His hands flew out to brace,
But mid the laughter of the crowd
He fell flat on his face.

So down he fell and with him hope
--He couldn't win it now--
Embarrassed, sad, he only wished
To disappear somehow.

But as he fell his dad stood up
And showed his anxious face,
Which to the boy so clearly said,
"Get up and win the race."

He quickly rose, no damage done,
--Behind a bit, that's all--
And ran with all his mind and might
To make up for his fall.

So anxious to restore himself
--To catch up and to win--
His mind went faster than his legs:
He slipped and fell again!

He wished then he had quit before
With only one disgrace.
"I'm hopeless as a runner now;
I shouldn't try to race."

But in the laughing crowd he searched
And found his father's face;
That steady look which said again:
"Get up and win the race!"

So up he jumped to try again
--Ten yards behind the last--
"If I'm to gain those yards," he thought,
"I've got to move real fast."

Exerting everything he had
He regained eight or ten,
But trying so hard to catch the lead
He slipped and fell again!

Defeat! He lay there silently
--A tear dropped from his eye--
"There's no sense running any more;
Three strikes: I'm out! Why try!"

The will to rise had disappeared;
All hope had fled away;
So far behind, so error prone;
A loser all the way.

"I've lost, so what's the use," he thought
"I'll live with my disgrace."
But then he thought about his dad
Who soon he'd have to face.

"Get up," an echo sounded low.
"Get up and take your place;
You were not meant for failure here.
Get up and win the race."

"With borrowed will get up," it said,
"You haven't lost at all.
For winning is no more than this:
To rise each time you fall."

So up he rose to run once more,
And with a new commit
He resolved that win or lose
At least he wouldn't quit.

So far behind the others now,
--The most he'd ever been--
Still he gave it all he had
And ran as though to win.

Three times he'd fallen, stumbling;
Three times he rose again;
Too far behind to hope to win
He still ran to the end.

They cheered the winning runner
As he crossed the line first place.
Head high, and proud, and happy;
No falling, no disgrace.

But when the fallen youngster
Crossed the line last place,
The crowd gave him the greater cheer,
For finishing the race.

And even though he came in last
With head bowed low, unproud,
You would have thought he'd won the race
To listen to the crowd.

And to his dad he sadly said,
"I didn't do too well."
"To me, you won," his father said.
"You rose each time you fell."

III

And now when things seem dark and hard
And difficult to face,
The memory of that little boy
Helps me in my race.

For all of life is like that race,
With ups and downs and all.
And all you have to do to win,
Is rise each time you fall.

"Quit! Give up! You're beaten!"
They still shout in my face.
But another voice within me says:
"GET UP AND WIN THE RACE!"

...Forgetting what is behind and straining toward what is ahead, I press on toward the goal to win the prize for which God has called me... – Philippians 3:13-14

For more information on booking Larry Hehn visit
www.larryhehn.com

Printed in the United States
90440LV00002B/4-18/A

9 781894 928267